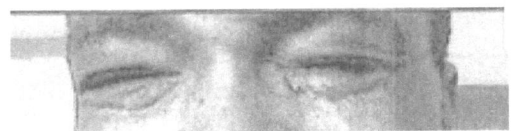

My Struggles,

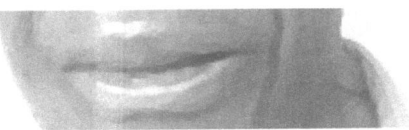

My Bondage,

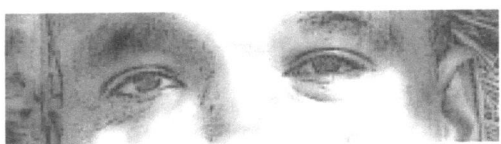

And My Freedom

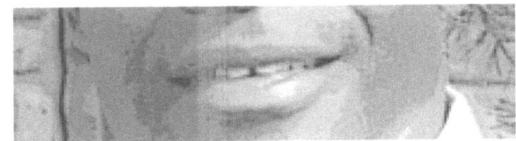

And Deliverance

Eddy Colin

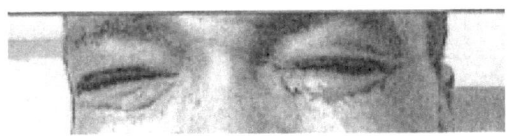

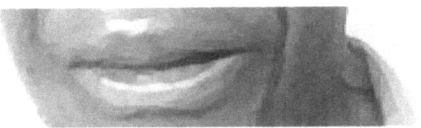

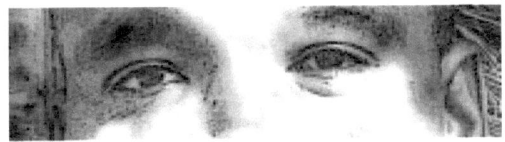

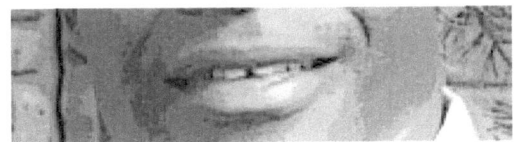

PUBLICATIONS, GRAPHICS & DESIGNS

Printed in the USA

ACKNOWLEDGMENTS

I would like to dedicate this manuscript to my mother, Clairia, and all the sacrifices that were made so I could be here and alive today. To my father Nicolas, who gave up everything and labored hard all his life to make sure we had an education. To my dearest brother Leon, who gave up all the education he could have had by dropping out of school very early in life to work side by side with my father so the rest of us children could eat and go to school to achieve what he himself could have easily achieved but gave it all up for us: thank you for giving up your life's dreams for me and I love you very much, brother. To my sister Nicole, who was always there for me, and who stayed up late with me making sure I understood my school work and finished all my homework. To my brother Hubert, and my dear brothers Smith and Claude, thank you so very much for all that you guys have done for me - you took care of me, and protected me from harm all my life. Mireille, I hope you can find your way home again because we all love you and miss you very much! Finally, to my sister and Godmother in Haiti, thank you for making it possible for me to have entered the United States of America, making it possible for me to become who I have become. Robin Bruce, my editor, God will bless you tremendously for helping me to accomplish my dream and God's work!!!

CONTENTS

This is

my story, your story,

our story.

Truly believe,

without any doubts,

it is time to be

rescued...

PROLOGUE

The journey

Twenty fourth of December two thousand seven was the last time that I stumbled and fell with my addiction to cocaine, when my God said, *Enough! Your struggles, I have seen. Your prayers, I have heard and answered. It is time to be rescued. I have only allowed the devil to believe that he was in control of your life for the greater good of mankind, in the same manner that he believed to have been in control when he had my son, your redeemer, Jesus Christ crucified on that rugged cross.*

I had my gun in my hands to kill myself, but a miracle took place as the Holy Spirit, whom God sent me, intervened and stopped me. After twenty six years of bondage and struggles from my cocaine addiction, God delivered me in an instant, without any doctors involved or any clinics for addiction. As I write this testimony — my testimony, your testimony, *our* testimony — free of all cocaine within my system and having no thoughts or desire for cocaine, I feel complete now.

My friends, the things that are happening in my life right now are so amazing that I don't know where to start. I just smile at everything — almost, because I have found a level of joy and comprehension which can only be appreciated and understood while being under the wings of Almighty God through the blood of Christ Jesus.

Having been awakened as I have been now, everything is not even close in resemblance to what I used to be like. My demeanor has changed, what I used to get overanxious about is no longer, and the manner in which I see time is totally different then I used to. In the past, if something was not going my way or if I did not get what I felt that I needed to have at any certain time, it would consume me somewhat thus creating the snowball effect in everything else that I was doing or going to do.

Now, our God is overwhelming me with all sorts of miracles. I found that by making God the center of everything that I do, He continually takes care of all my needs. The day I sold my only form of transportation in order to pay for the printing of this book was the first of many miracles. After one call to my good friend, he delivered a vehicle to my house, had four new tires installed on the vehicle, replaced the wiper assembly, plated it, and added insurance on it — just so I could have transportation back and forth to work and take care of my everyday affairs.

Then the screen on my laptop computer broke and the computer was operating improperly so I had no computer to transfer this manuscript to a document format. Another friend of mine found a new screen for me on eBay, repaired everything promptly, and did not charge me a dime, for the sake of this book. When I did not have a printer, not only did I get a printer, but I got a second very fast printer, brand new, from another friend for free, for the sake of this book.

Even my editor, at first a total stranger but who has been helping me from day one with the whole process (considering that I know nothing about publishing a book), after she got done reading the manuscript said that it made great reading and she would gladly go on my journey with me. She said she had been praying about it, and that God guided her to charge me very little to turn my manuscript into a book. **Now that is a miracle!!!!!!**

From everything that I am seeing and experiencing around me at this time, I am lead to truly believe that angels are among us constantly.

I love God so much that He has become the center of everything that I do in my life. This new found fountain of knowledge has made me the wealthiest man here on earth today (*So can you even imagine of the grander of what awaits for us in heaven. WOW!!!!!*). I am not speaking of the desire of the flesh or personal gains. I am speaking of genuine love, compassion toward others, and understanding regardless of how good, bad, or difficult things may get. And as I live my days here on this earth I shall be living proof of these words.

Being surrounded by the Divine as I am now,

living and abiding by all His rules and benefits, I surely believe to be the major key factor to my being in good health. In the morning when I awake, God is the first thing I think about. During the day, I think about Him almost constantly. At night, before I retire to bed, I make Him the last order of my business. Thus concludes my most perfect day. Only if there was a meter that could measure the feelings and effects and changes going on in my body right now could you truly understand.

Having understood this language of the age of enlightenment, I got to understand what my savior Jesus Christ meant about sending us a counselor who would reside within us, and who would guide us, and I am privileged to have the blessing of the Most High, my God, my creator. Furthermore, having the Holy Spirit within me at all times, I understand that the true purpose of my Counselor within me is our God given privilege, available to all of us and obtainable by all of us today and now.

But this road is being paved for *your* successful journey right now, if you are willing and ready to follow unselfishly. Even things that may be so grave where other people may not and cannot understand, you must find the compassion within you. Any obstacle that you encounter, is according to God's perfect will. Any success that you encounter, is according to God's perfect will. So learn to understand these things that will surely happen in all our lives and you will be well on your way on the path to your successful journey. I can say this because I now understand His ways better.

This day I pray that God will use me in a major way that the Holy Spirit, my counselor, will shine through me; that I may create a change in someone's life that will glorify our God for all that He has done for us; and that the person involved would be enlightened and feel the presence of the Almighty God in that moment and understand.

I am but a messenger and a servant of God, humbled and awakened at the days of enlightenment, to testify on behalf of my Creator of what is to come soon and express the urgency of what truly is at risk here and now...

May God open your hearts and minds to understand and accept these words as the truth. I look forward to your speedy response and thank you for your attention.

Sincerely yours.

Eddy Colin.

This is

my story, your story,

our story.

Truly believe,

without any doubts,

it is time...

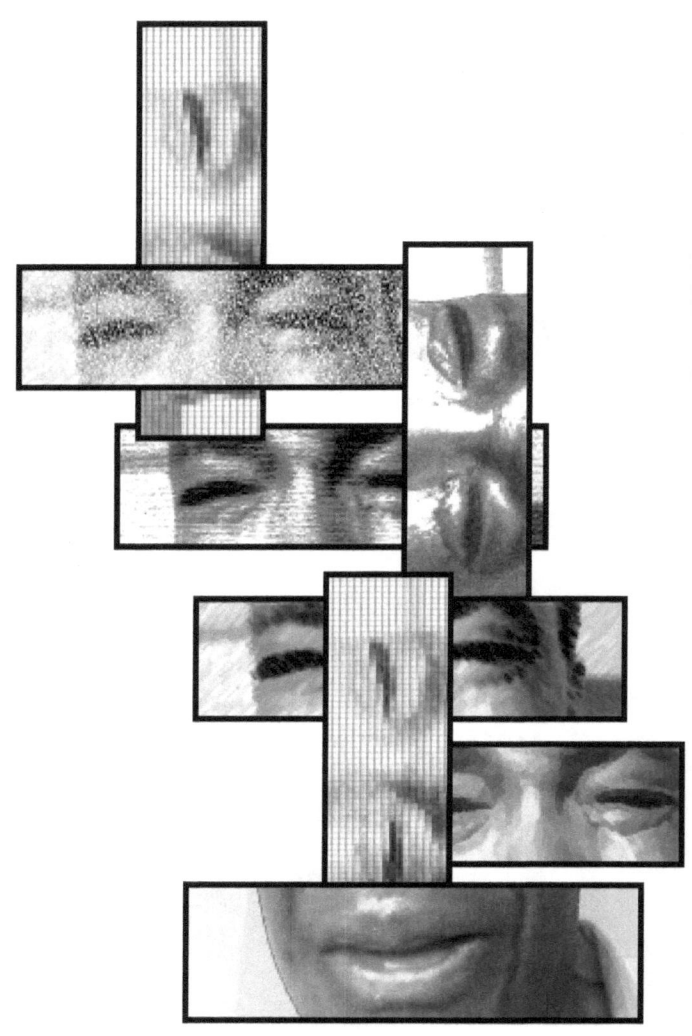

MY STORY

My struggles, my bondage, and my freedom and deliverance.

Dec. 25th, 2007
> The crossroads of it all.

The beginning of my understanding of what needs to be understood by me in my new journey, which is critical for me understanding the purpose at hand.

My thoughts are cloudy and yet very clear, but I know that I have been chosen to accomplish something that is now hard to understand. And the truth deep within my being is very clear, and from this moment forth I must continue to write this journal — for I know it is important. I don't know how I know this but I just do.

The roads that I must travel in my journey, I believe, are going to be difficult and I accept my quest into my destiny.

Most, even my loved ones, may not

understand and may not be able to follow me — but I understand.

No need for me to even attempt to forgive them because no forgiveness is necessary.

I know and I understand this is my road to travel and someday it will be <u>understood</u>: *within myself, "body and spirit," is the key to unlocking future mysteries. I don't know how and where all this is coming from but I know that I must write all this down.

I know that I am not losing my mind — I just know. We are still very closed minded as human beings. Marijuana, for instance, was looked upon as illegal and bad for you but now it is being used in the medical practices with cancer patients.

Different time to learn different things.

All these thoughts I am having now is partially when I am on cocaine, and I can feel God reaching in. I know this is very important, and that is why I am putting it all on paper now, because it's time for the truth.

As I write these things down, I can feel a force trying to keep me from doing this. There is a whole other language, a whole other level of communication, much more and much higher then we know. In time, in time, in time. We will eventually understand. We are at the dawn of a new age, a new evolution in the works, but we must be careful of how we interpret these thoughts. They must be extremely positive and good, for it is the right way.

I now know for sure I have been granted this gift, and I have been delivered from the beast of an addiction. This is my story, your story, our story.

My struggle, my bondage, my deliverance.

The pain and agony within my inner self is so great, it hurts constantly. I now understand why God in the beginning was trying to keep Adam and Eve from the tree of knowledge of good and evil. I want the world to know that these thoughts, I believe, to be a guide for all to follow, in order to become whole and understand what roads they may have to travel to win this fight and gain their deliverance from the bondage of the adversary in our world today.

I must surround myself with the divine light of God "Jehovah" to remain safe at all times, for I am constantly under attack by evil forces.

My friends, Jesus fought the ultimate battle for us and won, but there is a whole new battle we must fight and win ourselves with God's help.

First we must surround ourselves with the armor of God. His divine light must be around us always.

I prayed to my creator in agony, as a child of light, to rescue me over and over and over again because I got to the point of no return — I thought. But my God knows best.

God will let us use our free will to whatever depth necessary to mold us and save us. I now understand what God was saying when he said: "I will never leave you nor forsake you." For even when I felt all alone, I was under his wings.

This is a new age we are living in. We must learn not to judge so quickly, instead learn to understand more and more at all cost. Only then can we ourselves be free.

In my solitude, it is so overwhelming the feelings that I can finally understand, and without a doubt, I can tell you it is of the unconditional love of God my father; and being in this sad yet very peaceful place, I can almost speak this language that I am being taught by the higher powers.

My friends, this is the ultimate peace in knowing and experiencing a stillness beyond anything known to most. And the best part of it all is knowing that I have been delivered from my addiction through the blood of Christ Jesus.

The love surrounding my being is so thick that I get the chills through my entire body, as the thoughts are pouring out, as if I was being dictated by someone whispering not in my ears but the center part of my brain (top of my head, center brain area). Everything is so clear in my mind's eyes. Never before have I been so clear about what I must do.

I truly believe, without any doubts, that this book has to be written right now and my testimony needs to be told for the enlightenment and the deliverance of all who are ready and will listen to their hearts.

For as long as I can remember, since I was a young boy, I kept having this reoccurring dream. It was as if I were being shown many important things by, what I want to refer to as, my guide and as if I had no body — just being there as air is, or the molecules around us, etc... etc...

It would fly me around through different stages of things that they wanted to show me. First thing was the deep blue, where I encountered things that I still can't explain. Second, an old way of life of a certain Indian tribe, very, very ancient. I was taken through their habitat, within their dwellings, and how they lived — simplicity yet complex — their water distribution, farming, living quarters etc... etc...

Third, a war that arrived here on Earth, and with the technology of the unknown adversary, we had no chance. Fourth, they took me back to where I believe my great-great-grandparents lived as slaves on a plantation in Haiti, and all had been burnt and destroyed. But every time I would have one of these "dreams" as we call them, I would end up in front of an ocean, body of water. I would be let down right there and unable to cross, and it (my guide) would be gone already.

Finally in the end, my last and final dream, was when they again showed me my great-great- grandparents' slave plantation burnt and destroyed. As I was being shown that, I got to that same ocean and finally, for the first time, they took me across that ocean and let me down on a safe cliff side like the same Indian dwellings from one of my previous dreams. They told me, *You will never see me again*, as if my own journey was to start.

Those dreams started when I was about maybe late teens or early twenties, and they stopped in my early to mid thirties.

No coincidence here. I believe that all this has a role in how this book will shape up. Why do I believe this? I just do.

You must embrace your life's journey because while here on earth, you only have one life, one shot. Until we acknowledge and embrace the whole world as our brothers and sisters, as our mothers and fathers, etc., etc., we will fall short in accomplishing what truly needs to be and have complete peace, love, harmony, and tranquility as it was all designed to be by our Creator, the designer and maker of it all.

We must embrace all people, no matter what, and try our hardest to understand. Remember one thing, they too have their journey and all end up in the same place in the end. The more and more we accept them and understand them, the closer we will be to the point of what it was supposed to be like from the beginning of our creation.

My brothers and sisters, we have the power within us right now to end world hunger, homelessness and much more to start with. But until we can get rid of our selfish nature within us, we cannot accomplish this task which is very simple to do.

For example, millions of super rich hold on to their every dime, money that can't be used or spent in five, ten, twenty of their life times. Why?.... How much money does one person need to live in one life?

And I am not saying to just throw money away, or just give money away just to give it away. Imagine a world where everyone willingly help others, help one another, and work together with the one common goal. There would be no poor, and no rich as we know it *(but rich indeed)*, no homeless, no hunger, etc., etc.

My dear friends, brothers and sisters, this book is no simple book yet it is very simple. You must open yourselves to limitless possibilities for the [sake] of our future as a civilization.

This book will be our today guide to accomplish what ancient civilizations have accomplished already. How do I know this? I just do. Even when the devil pulled me down into the deepest pits, in my worst agony, I was in my prayers and still had clear focus on my God. Not ever had my God left me alone or forsook me.

They are your most powerful weapons in the universe: your faith, your belief, and your prayers. No matter what, never stop, for the answer will come surely.

I have never in my whole life been so certain of what these words that I must write down are all about. *[]*I believe by writing this book, too many people will know the truth about the adversary and I am exposing him for what he is — a "liar."

I am writing *[this]* within seconds of coming out of my dream. It is exactly 3:15 a.m. (looking at cell phone screen), now December the 29th. Brothers and sisters, I am now under serious attack by evil forces of a different level. I want you to believe me when I say to you, the time has come 100% and we all need to surround ourselves with the light, the divine light of God, to remain safe from now on. And those of us who will play a big part in this battle must remain always under the wings of God.

*[]*Last night, December twenty eight two thousand seven, I sat in the recliner and watched the weather, the Letterman Show, and retired to bed. As if immediately, I went into a whole new dream. *[]*In my dream, as if I was an observer and yet, I played a part in what I believe to be the preparation of a spiritual warfare. I saw a place within an ancient sanctuary and a sealed chamber, like a spirit that had been locked away got out. And I had no fear anymore, for my strong belief and strength in God/Jesus is clearer then ever. I was able to protect those around me in one statement *(for God to surround me and all the rest of us with his divine light and protect us)* as this particular spirit was sealed in for good reasons. Immediately upon asking my God to shield us with his divine light, the spirit was sucked back into that chamber and resealed.

Phase two of the dream: We got to a destination unclear to me. As I preached to the group on how different things were going to be from now on, and how they must stay in the light, suddenly my bed was rocking vigorously. As I was trying to wake up, I felt as if I was being pressed down in my bed. I felt a very thick and furious presence in between my dream and my room/bed with me. It took all my strength as I prayed to God in a panic, to protect me and surround me with his divine light. And it was done. After I came to, completely awake, the evil presence was still there in the room. With tears in my eyes, heart pounding and my voice trembling, I demanded in the name of Jesus, who empowered me, for the spirit to be gone and leave *now*. In a split second, almost instantly, it fled and was gone.

It saddens me so much and I am so overwhelmed by such intense sadness as I try to maintain and not cry. I feel as if time is critical for this book.

This day I took off from work, free of all drugs and alcohol of course, and I commit myself to continue to write for as long as I am being dictated through my mind. As the rest of the world continues in its today routine, I will dedicate myself to this mission at hand, for I know I must.

My friends, I Eddy Colin, have never felt as whole, as complete, and as free as I am feeling right now. I now understand why I needed to go through everything that God has allowed me to have gone through.

Although as human beings, our minds have been conditioned by the adversary to accept selfishness as one of our traits [and] we can't see with our mind's eyes anymore. No matter how big, and how bad of what we are going through, God has a plan. Helping one another should come as natural as breathing. Only then can we have the peace that God intended. One thing that I know for a fact is that God's word is very much alive — as alive as I am here today, writing this book as my testimony and as a guide for all whose time have come to be delivered and be freed from the bondage of the adversary in our world today.

Please!!!! My brothers and sisters, you must open your hearts and your minds to these words that I have been commissioned to pass on to you; to discover how real and powerful our God is and how alive He still is as He was in the beginning.

He said in time of trouble, when you need Him the most, that He will be there for us and that "never" will He leave us or forsake us.

My friends, I tell you today that no man has helped me with my addiction of drugs and alcohol — not the doctors, not my friends, and not my closest family and loved ones.

I got to my lowest point in my life, with my gun in my hand, *[and]* before I was able to pull the trigger, the Holy Spirit, my counselor, intervened and stopped me. Finally even one of my loved ones gave up on me. But at my lowest point, when I needed my God the most, on my knees I called him on his promised words to me and I was delivered once and for all.

As I write these words now with tears pouring out of my eyes, *[sitting]* on my bed, I have never been happier and I have never been so free as I am feeling right now, for the grace of God has been poured upon me. These tears of joy I want you all to know are for my deliverance from the bondage from the adversary. Glory be to God!!!!!!!!!!!!!!!!!!

The devil is extremely smart and knows every trick in his book to hold us down — especially when we are trying to shed light on his lies. But in my case, all he ended up doing is giving me all the ammunition I needed for this book, which will in turn shed light on his lies and give the readers more ammunition to face him. For, this is the book of enlightenment.

Deep within my being, [] God planted within me the knowledge that He had a great purpose for me, and I have always felt it and known it. My dear friends, God is very much alive. He has a plan for all of us, and all you have to do is believe in his words and follow the right and true roads. He will guide you if you listen closely, you will recognize His voice. And no matter how difficult the terrains may get, you must continue to lean on your God because He has always loved you and will never leave you nor forsake you, ever. Take my word for it. I am living proof of it and I am writing this book.

This is the age of enlightenment. Follow your dreams and listen to your thoughts — they are very real. It is its own language and don't let yourselves think otherwise. What I feel of this unconditional love is that what my God has for me is so overwhelming, that mere words cannot explain it. It is that language which you can only feel in your heart and soul and I believe that this is a new age, the age of enlightenment of which I am being told about right now. After this book has been read by many, we as a civilization will start seeing the changes in our world. For I know it is our destiny. I don't know how I know, I just do.

These words as I write them down are exactly as I am being dictated to write them. I no longer question my instinct and my feelings, for I know the truth more then ever now.

I am completely surrounded by the divine light at all times so I can be shielded and protected. And I fear no evil, for God is with me always. I feel as if I am slowly entering in complete harmony with the positive forces from a dimension I don't yet understand one hundred percent, but I know this for a fact: that I am the beginning of a new creation of the age of enlightenment. What ever is to come from the writing of these words, I accept, for my God is with me always.

Pray for me my friends.

I was born and raised in Port-au-Prince, Haiti, a small french/creole speaking island in the Caribbean. I am the eighth of eight children and against all odds I was born. My mother almost died giving birth to me, for she was told by doctors not to have anymore children or she may not come out of it alive.

As a kid I was always trying to make sense out of everything as if there was a missing piece or part of a puzzle. I would lay by myself on our roof at night sometimes and look into the heavens and would try my hardest to figure things out. I had people around me and yet I always felt so alone, and my heart felt empty as if something was missing.

My father worked extremely hard to put food on the table, and I remember times almost the whole day had elapsed and my poor mother still did not know how, or what, or if she would be able to feed us that day. Finally it would be time for supper and my mother would go completely hungry, maybe just one piece of bread for her so we may have just a little bit more in our stomachs for supper, our one and only meal that day. I could see the pain in her eyes so vividly as my stomach hurt from my hunger pangs. As you can see, God picked me before I even knew that today I would be writing these words down about world hunger and how we as a civilization can stop it. My friends, that type of hunger is not by choice at all, it is a way of life for many. The forces of evil is as real as you are seeing and reading these words today.

The voodoo religion is real in Haiti as I have sat as a kid in ceremonies and witnessed it's power. My friends, these stories I am about to tell you are real. I was there and I got them first hand from these spirits/entities. I know of three names that I can remember: dambala, papa legba, ezulie. These are the names of the three that I can remember.

First story:
Every time there was a ceremony, these

spirits would always ask for me to come and
[sit] by them, since I would always ask lots
of questions as they would give me answers.
The one question that I ask them that stayed
with me until now was, "Who are you and
where did you come from?" In order for
them to give me an answer, they had to go
back to the beginning when they were good
and trusted angels in heaven, including
Lucifer one of the most trusted angels by
God. They told me that Lucifer had planned
a coup d'etat in heaven and had many angels
on his side, somehow including them, and it
was unsuccessful so they all got thrown out
of heaven by God never to return. Many
ended up here on earth and most of them are
very, very bad still with Lucifer, and they still
have all their powers. They can only enter
our realm when we invite them, not knowing
what we are doing.

Others like dambala, legba, and ezulie chose
families like my family and adopted them.
They would help us when we are sick and
stuff and when attacked by evil forces, they
would protect us. They told me that they are
trying to keep doing good so when it's all
said and done, knowing how merciful our

God is, that maybe they would have a chance at returning home in heaven and they regretted what they have done.

Second story:
My brother, [the] first born, was very ill on his death bed. My sister had a dream that the next day at high noon, when things were just right, that a spirit would come and claim my brother's life. That was the first time as a young boy that I witness the power of God. We were told that there was one way and only one way to save my brother once and for all. We were all to hold hands, on our knees, around his bed and recite a certain prayer over and over again.

My dear friends, that day God was alive then and is still alive and on his throne today. At high noon, we all started reciting that prayer together and the battle between God and evil started. I was there flesh and blood as God is my witness. My brother's bed started shaking and vibrating vigorously and lifted off the floor some. As things got more and more intense we kept reciting that prayer non stop and, after a few minutes, it all came to a stop. On that day the power of God prevailed once more and my brother was saved.

Third story:
My sister was very smart in school, and in her college years she had a close friend, but the friend was always jealous of how smart my sister was. One night, my sister had a dream that her friend would bring a book for her to read; and in the dream, they told her when the book comes, not to read it and if she did read that book, she would go blind, and that there would be only one way to reverse the effect of her blindness — our family dog would have to be sacrificed. And the dream ended. Sure enough the next day as her dream predicted, her friend brought her a book to read. At that time my sister did not even think of her dream [n]or remembered. She started reading the book, immediately she went blind. Suddenly she remembered her dream.

It's now about mid afternoon, my father came home and learned of what had happened to my sister, but also knew about my sister's dream. They all decided no way, not our family dog, there must be another way, there has to be. Considering that my family had never been part of anything like that before, so my father decided to go in the country to find my uncle, a voodoo priest, to try to fix things. We made sure that our family dog was inside the house and safe.

All of a sudden, as my dad was leaving the driveway to go get my uncle, the dog ran out of the house, under the tire of my dad's vehicle and was killed. As soon as the dog dies, my sister regained her vision as it was before she read that book. Unexplained but true.

Fourth and last story:
That same sister I now believe to be a voodoo priestess and carrying the family torch. As you know, Haiti is in political chaos and turmoil. A group of guerilla fighters/goons were sent to my sister's neighborhood to kill many people including my sister. When they got to her house, in front, she somehow immediately went into a trance and all these fighters saw were many armed guards protecting her house. Believe me when I say this to you, there were no armed guards there (it is what was projected

by my sister somehow in her trance for these
fighters to see).

All my life, I have always felt that something
was missing, like a void at the bottom of
your stomach and in your heart, and I finally
feel complete and I know why I can feel so
whole and so complete now. It is because I
have been building up to this story about my
life that had not been told yet, because it was
not yet complete and was not ready to be
told.

We must be patient. We must allow God to
mold us for what he will have us do for him,
for ourselves; because in the end, it will be
our own destiny that will have been fulfilled.
I am so excited to be part of something so
big. As you will find out, ultimately God is
the captain of this ship, and He will help you
get home safe.

As you are reading this book, you will notice
that there are no reference numbers out of
the Bible. It is because this is all just coming
to me and I write down what I am being
dictated to write down. God's hand is very
much in this book and he has never started

any project in our entire history that was left unfinished. And if anybody could find one right now it would only mean that it is not time for it to be finished yet. God has all the time in the world because he created it.

This is so important to me, that out of the blue as if someone told me that it was time for this book to be written. I have a good job, and as of four days ago, I just stopped going to work and started writing; and I have not stopped but to eat and [to drink] water/ tea, other than that I have just been working on this book. I remember they say that in Noah's time, before the big flood, the people thought that he was a crazy old man. Was he crazy? Hummmm? My dear friends we better start listening to our hearts and our thoughts, for the time is closer than then you think.

If I never accomplish another thing in this life time, this book will have been all worth it for I believe, without a shadow of a doubt, that this book is about to deliver many who are so afraid to express what is truly going on in their lives. I know because I was one of those people.

All my tears have been wiped out, my addiction to cocaine has been eradicated, and my selfish nature has been erased; and from this moment forward, I will surrender my entire life to Jesus Christ.

If you listen for your shepherd's voice, you will always hear it — that is if you really want to hear it — and he will always lead you to safety.

Something that took the devil twenty six years to put together was destroyed by my God in an instant. My addiction has taken the adversary twenty six years to bury me in the deepest pit, and he is so talented at deceptions that he puts the most interesting people in my life to cheer me on and support me. But the agonies with my bondage was well worth it, for it will help bring thousands and thousands to Christ through this book.

Today, December the thirtieth, for the first time in many years, my freedom took me to Mission Hill Church, *Hallelujah!*, as if God himself took me there, and my family in Christ Jesus were waiting to meet with me and greet me. Many of the staff, including the pastor, welcomed me with open arms. At the end of the service, many came to talk with me, showed genuine interest in me as if God had already prepared their hearts to receive me and accept me as one of their own. As I have said before, if you listen to your shepherd's voice, you will always hear it, "if you really want to."

I see today as the beginning of a brand new life with endless possibilities. My friends, if you have any doubts what so ever about what God can do for you in your life, I want to stop you right now for just a moment. After reading about my twenty six years of bondage and struggles, and how God delivered me in an instant without any doctors involved or any clinics for addiction, shouldn't you believe that there is no task too big for God?

I know that God has called me to testify on His behalf about how much He cares for us, how much He really loves us; and what ever it takes, I will rearrange my entire life, at all cost, to testify and witnessed for the greatest cause of all.

This book is nothing short of a true miracle from God for our age to know about, and not even the devil can make a miracle from God go unnoticed and be overlooked when God puts His foot down and tells the devil to step aside for His people to receive His words.

How do we explain why a forty seven year old professional man wakes up one day, quits his job, and feels that he got a call from God, that it was time for a book that he believes God has commissioned him to write because it is time? I have not been at work since December the 24th, 2007, a total of nine days now under the guidance of God, and I will finally finish this book.

And to prove to the world of how powerful God is, my vision from God is that Oprah Winfrey will be the person who will help start whispering this testament to God's people and you will surely know that these words are of God, my Father. As I work to get my story out, one of the news agencies told me that it was not worthy of a news story - good luck. How did we allow ourselves to come to this point?

Saturday, about 1:12 a.m., January the 5th, 2008. Just woke up from being asleep and, of course, free of all cocaine within my system now for twelve days since my deliverance from the beast. These early morning hours, normally I would still be up and would probably be very high on cocaine and drunk. But now, being so full of life and free from my struggles and my bondage, God has given me new reasons to live. So, instead of high and drunk, I write more testimonies so others may know more truths.

The truth is that until God created a real miracle in my life, I had never gone more than two, maybe three, days off the cocaine. It is so clear to me now of what God has called me to do, and I am so privileged to have been chosen to represent the best of the best. And I am so anxious to start going across the United States into schools, prisons, shelters and rehabilitation places, even other countries — anywhere my call from God wants to take me and win lost and disoriented souls for Jesus Christ by sharing my testimony. The rest of my life belongs to God, for the cause is so great.

In that dream, when I felt as if I was preaching and preparing for a spiritual warfare, it is clearer to me now that I need to start using my testimony to win more souls for the army of God, because I know that the time is closer than ever.

My friends, if you ever experience a negative or unclean thought, know for sure, without any doubts, that it is from the adversary. Remember when I said that you must surround yourself with the armor of God, and that Jesus already fought the ultimate battle and won? He also empowered us through his death on the cross, to repel the devil at any of these times. And our counselor, the Holy Spirit, will always let us know the right from the wrong. Don't doubt yourselves ever because if you think and feel that it is wrong, that is because *it is wrong* and the devil is nearby whispering in your ears. So you must immediately exercise your right of empowerment, given to you by our savior and redeemer Jesus Christ, and demand in Jesus' name for the devil to be gone and he must go, and will go. Believe me, I know.

If for twenty six years I was able to carry on from a mere salesman at an auto dealership and work my way up to running auto dealerships, making important decisions everyday which impact many lives, and knowing that many of those decisions were made with cocaine in my system from the previous night and, without any doubts, a very cloudy mind, it scares me a lot thinking that with the level of our technology today in the world, that here are hundreds of thousands of people with addiction to hard drugs and therefore cloudy minds — how safe are we all?

This why I know for a fact that this manuscript will play a major role in diffusing this time bomb which has been planted by the adversary, "**the devil**."

Now that the veil of clouds has been lifted and removed from my eyes, thus allowing me to see things as Jesus would have if he were walking the earth as we know it and live on it today, I can vividly see that we are in the need of godly/divine intervention right away; for we have reached the critical zone and many, many souls are at stake.

God has prepared me extremely well and carefully molded me for this mission at hand. I write these words carefully so you may get a glimpse of what he is showing you through me. I say to you today and now, this may be the last chance of grace and redemption for you for this door is about to be closed, and once closed, there will be no more hope for you ever. You have been given another chance through these words of truth and enlightenment. Seize this opportunity of a life time, of your life, to secure your eternity with your creator. As I have mentioned earlier in this manuscript: there is a big storm coming and to survive this storm, there is only one way. And that is to seek shelter under God's wings. So my friends, don't get caught in this storm without shelter for it may be too late if you don't act now.

I have found that there is only person that you can truly count on every time, all the time, for He remains the same always, has never changed throughout time, and will be the same for eternity to come. He is pure love, and wisdom. You must follow your heart with the God-kind of love and wisdom, knowing right from wrong since He already gifted you with that knowledge.

As I now can speak this language which I have referred to in the manuscript, so will you: be able to hear his voice, listen and understand this language. All this can only happen to you if your motives and reasons are one hundred percent unselfish and some, for this is one thing which cannot be manipulated. I will say to you that this is godliness for I can feel, speak, and understand this language. Being a servant against one's will is wrong, but to understand and be [a] servant of God willingly is the greatest accomplishment one could ever accomplish. For it leads you to the ultimate peace that we have all been searching for. And it truly starts with surrendering to Christ Jesus who is the way and the truth.

This has been the testimony of my struggles, my bondage, my freedom, and my deliverance by Christ Jesus.

This is

my story, your story,

our story.

Truly believe,

without any doubts...

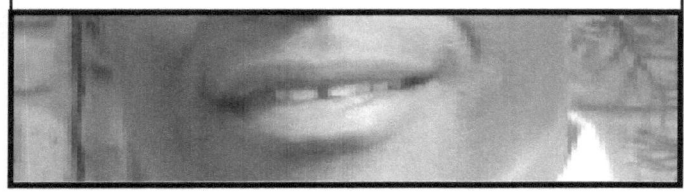

EPILOGUE

The deliverance

I wanted to conclude this book pages ago,
but that is precisely what I am talking about,
our God knows best. We cannot rush God,
for He knows every time what is the perfect
time table for everything. When He is done
dictating to me and says it is finished, then it
will be.

Being guided by the Holy Spirit, my
counselor, as I am being guided now, I will
say to you my friend that something of great
importance and value is taking place right
now in these days of enlightenment; and I
beg of you to repent and come under His
grace right now, for the window of
opportunity will not stay open permanently.

Once you have been delivered, everything
will be totally different in your life.
Unimaginable things, occurrences, miracles,
etc., etc., will take place in your life. And the
doubts will still come into your mind but the
Holy Spirit, your counselor, is now within

you as one, thus allowing you to move in the right directions and make decisions perfectly, where normally you would stumble and fall. When you understand finally how God operates, good or bad, it's all good.

The roads have already been paved for you to enter into His kingdom/your home that His son, your redeemer and personal savior, has been preparing just for you. This, your inheritance, has been promised to you and predicted by the prophets of ancient times.

Unfortunately there are no shortcuts for you to get to where I am now in my position of privilege with God. It can only be obtained through trials and much needed discipline, and, by the grace of God, you have been given a glimpse at your future destiny.

Everything that you are going through right now, He understands and He wants you to know that you are not alone. And He will carry you when you are not able to continue this walk. You must continue to believe and have faith in Him, for He has always loved you and will continue to love you for eternity to come.

Brothers and sisters, this kind of understanding and love is very different, much deeper than any love or understanding you have ever experienced. Most people may never get there unless they stay in their prayers constantly, and I am speaking of true unconditional love from deep within.

Once you have surrendered to Christ and understand how it truly works, it will shed light on all that was unknown to you. You will start experiencing feelings, and really see how deep the love that God has for you is, and why you will need to stay in the light.

You will find out that God is an amazing god if you take the time to really get to know Him. He will give you more than you can ever imagine in your life but you must give up most of the unnecessary things, if not all, that the adversary has taught you throughout your lifetime here on earth are important. Remember the devil is a liar and a master at misrepresentation of things carnal.

And you also must pray constantly. For the adversary will want to "try" to stop you because he knows that the more times something like this happens, that's less soldiers for his army. And he also knows that time is drawing very near for the big battle between good and evil.

My friends, God has revealed to you the ultimate pathway to achieve eternal life and He has used me as an agent of his to help you see what your true future is. As you try to make this decision, the adversary, the devil, will try to stop you because he is about to lose you to God forever and he gets very mad whenever he loses a person to God. So stay firm in your belief and your prayers.

God still does miracles and He is as alive today as He ever was. I quit my job for a while to pursue my new journey. That is how much I believe in what this manuscript will do for all of us. My book is non-fiction and is of God. I know that God is now ready to answer all your unselfish prayers as a result of your enlightenment from this manuscript!!!!!!!!!!!!!!

This is

my story, your story,

our story.

Truly believe...

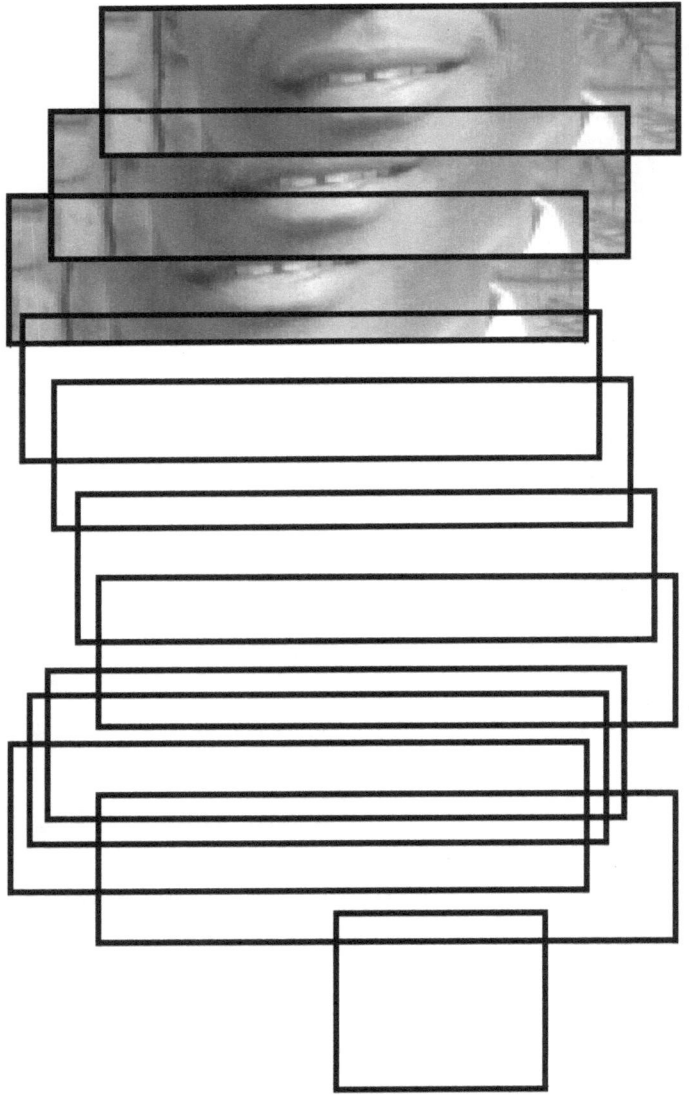

YOUR STORY

The testimony:

This is so exiting that I can't even make myself stop writing. All this is coming at me like an open stream of water. So you can have an idea of how well nourished I am with these words. It is three ten in the morning, February the eighteenth, two thousand eight. I am still very much clean from the cocaine addiction and am totally in control of my life now with the help from the divine God.

Everyday of my life I will give praise to God, for without him I am nothing. My life is such now that I could not imagine, or even consider, not being under His wings. He is so very much alive my friends. Seize this opportunity and get to know Him through my testimonies, and write your own testimony so you can make a difference in other lives as I am in yours.

As I have been saying and trying to help you understand, this book is no simple book yet it is and should be the easiest book to understand, for it is the book of enlightenment given to you through me as a revelation from the Most High. Every now and then, God will reveal of what is to come in its own time to a person and He will guide that person, may even allow that person to go through horrible trials, but it is all for the greater good of mankind. Only what you can handle will He allow you to endure. That is why the words and statements in this manuscript are revealed to you at this time.

Coincidence? Not a chance. He knows exactly why and what He has in store for you because He is pure love and wisdom.

There have been many who have perished, many who have given their lives willingly, so I was born. And those who had done that, did not even know about this big picture today of which I am unveiling to you. I cannot express enough the urgency of this to make you understand as I do, of how critical it is for all to accept these words as gospel and abide by them, for your eternal salvation depends on it.

I can only imagine of the grander of this, of

what will be when this is all understood by most of us. And having all the earth — this earth — operating at one hundred percent with no more chains, with all struggles gone, and bondage erased once and for all. My goodness, can you just visualize what I am seeing right now?

You can make a difference in other lives. Seize this opportunity. Tell your story.

This is

my story, your story,

our story.

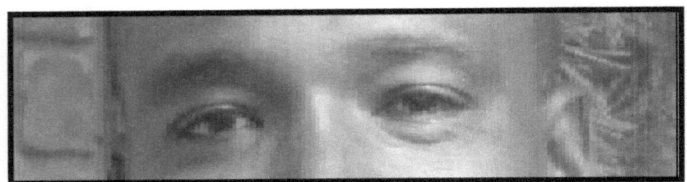

YOUR JOURNEY

Statements of truth to live by for a successful journey:

(1) I am the way, I am the truth, pick your cross and follow Me.

(2) I will never leave you, I will never forsake you.

(3) When you need Me the most, I will be there for you.

(4) My sheep know My voice, listen closely and you will hear Me.

(5) Where ever you are, there I will be.

(6) I created you, I have not changed, why have you changed so much?

(7) Now is the time, listen to the Counselor within you.

(8) You know My voice. Why won't you

acknowledge Me? For I planted the truth within you long ago.

(9) The storm that will come, no one will withstand unless they seek shelter under My wings.

(10) Your true destiny can only be fulfilled through my Son, and He is the only gateway through which you can get there.

(11) Listen to your heart, remember to follow your dreams.

(12) God heard your prayers and knows your struggles, so keep your faith alive for a special blessing is coming your way.

(13) You were born in the light, and you have the power within you to extinguish and illuminate this darkness.

(14) Act now. For tomorrow may be too late.

(15) I have accepted you as you are, why won't you accept Me?

(16) Within you is the knowledge of right and wrong. Listen to your heart for your Counselor is within you as my Son promised.

(17) To discover the power within you and how big My plan for you is, you must surrender all to my Son. Only then can you be complete and have peace.

(18) Understanding the many sacrifices made by others, from the Son of God on the cross redeeming you with His life/death to Christians killed, so that you would know God's plan for you is the first positive step toward your freedom and deliverance from the adversary.

(19) Pray unselfishly to God and believe in His son's death for your sins and you will surely be blessed.

(20) You can't experience and enjoy the magnitude of God's grace for you until you surrender all to his Son.

(21) Life without Jesus can never be

complete, and without Him in your life, eternity in love is at stake.

(22) Reading this book is the beginning of your transformation through Christ. And it will be the absolute best thing that will ever happen to you, and the start of your own new journey.

(23) There is no greater fulfillment then understanding finally the true nature of God, and on a personal level of relationship with the Creator, and truly know what our lord Jesus was speaking of.

(24) Writing this book is like kick starting a perpetual machine that will continue to run perpetually. And remember, our God is perpetual and He gave me this book to write. So you must write your own testimony as you get enlightened.

(25) The things that God can and will do for you in your life without repayment back to Him, no one on earth would even consider doing for you. This is a good time to start in your prayers. For God knows your heart and

He wants so badly to be part of your life because He loves you so much. That's why He sent His one and only Son to redeem you with His life giving for you on the cross so you may be saved once and for all. But you must surrender to his Son as your personal savior. Only then can you see the miracles that He can perform in your life.

(26) Through Christ, all is possible. It's no coincidence that this book is in your hands. Jesus is appealing to you to come back to Him. For His gift to you is eternal life with your Creator.

(27) All in this world are temporary — invest in the things that are eternal, with returns beyond your understanding. Put it all on God and have an eternally secured future.

(28) If at any time an unclean or untrue thought enters your mind, immediately ask God for guidance and for the intervention of your Counselor, the Holy Spirit, to minister to you in faith.

(29) The things of this world today are not

worth sacrificing your eternal soul for.
Continually pray in faith and confidence and
ask for guidance from the Holy Spirit in the
name of Jesus.

And remember: "Jesus Christ is the answer
and the way."

This is my story...

TWO YEARS LATER

At the age of forty-eight, I have finally made it to where I don't have to wonder anymore about why I am here on earth. I have been given the privilege to be the writer that I have become not by my own accord but by the grace of God, for the mission at hand is more important then all the treasures that the adversary has been placing before me as enticement in order to dissuade me from what is real and pure in the face of God, our creator.

Since my deliverance two years ago, my belief has risen to a level beyond anything that I could have ever understood before my freedom and deliverance from the adversary's bondage. My faith in my Creator, my God, is stronger than anything that I have ever felt in my entire life. I harmoniously walk with the Holy Spirit, my counselor, my guide, and one set of footprints is all you will see in the sand for we are as one. My God has taught me how to unconditionally love Him and others and everything that He stands for without the battle that most would go through from within. He is pure love, the kind of love that would be incomprehensible by most.

Being guided by the Holy Spirit is the most amazing feeling that one can ever experience. I am discovering all the potentials that have always been within me, potentials that I could not use or understand before my deliverance.

Back in about the year nineteen ninety four, with all the partying, the using, and the drinking, and all the stress of the long hours of the car business, I was found to have extremely high blood pressure. As my life insurance company was doing a physical, they discovered that I was at a "stage two hypertension" and I was told to make an appointment to go see my doctor as soon as possible. Since then, I had been on blood pressure medications every day, but three months or so after I got delivered from my struggles and my bondage from my addiction to cocaine, my God also delivered me from the high blood pressure and now, without any prescribed medication whatsoever, my blood pressure is running normal to high normal, and all I take daily are natural vitamins and minerals. I feel better than ever with God as the captain.

Yet my journey after my deliverance has not been an easy one but (my faith in God got me through). In the following pages, I will share my thoughts and trials along this journey, beginning back in 2008 I wrote:

As hard as it is sometimes, and as much as it hurts to lose a loved one, and even when we must give up the things that are dear to us, God is still in control and on His throne. Now more than ever, I understand what it means when God said I will never leave you nor forsake you; it means unconditionally I will always make sure all your needs are met simply because you abide by all My codes of ethics planted within you, and you know that all your debts to the adversary have been paid in full by My son as planned. So, rejoice and rejoice as you are My own creation.

I have only one mission in life now and it is simply to live and abide by all that is good in the eyes of God and I don't even have to try hard anymore because it has become second nature for me. I know and I can feel the presence of the Holy Spirit/my counselor within me, guiding me in every and all my decisions everyday now.

This day, April the 5th, 2008, the devil finally gave up on trying to entice me with cocaine, for he finally realizes that it does not work for me anymore as my thought process is completely guided by the Holy Spirit. He is pulling out of his bag of tricks now. People whom I believe to have been on my side through all this, including moral support while I have been working on this book, have now turned against me, calling names and referring to me as the devil, pushing verbally in extremely negative ways and trying to get under my skin to anger me. They have pushed me so hard but, through all that, I got calmer and calmer. I can feel the presence of the Holy Spirit within as vividly as a fresh breeze making contact with my skin on a cool summer day.

These days now, I feel the presence of God within and with me always, and I no longer feel guilty about anything I do anymore for I know one hundred percent that I am being guided by my counselor, the Holy Spirit, and more than ever I can separate right from wrong.

Furthermore I don't live for men anymore but for my God. I have found that most people only do things to benefit themselves almost all the time. And those same people don't even think twice about their behaviors, for they have totally been conditioned by the adversary to accept their behaviors as normalcy. They also acknowledge all others who are in higher levels and positions then they, thus establishing and creating what they believe to be a safer environment and possibly a more opportunistic life-style. They would do and go through almost anything. Being that dependent upon any mere man will get you nowhere secured.

Seeing these things happening right in front of my eyes now makes me love my God even more, and most of all: how secured I truly am under the wings of the Almighty God.

And He is with me always, and I know for a fact that He will never leave me nor forsake me, which has been proven over and over again in my life. Since my deliverance, financially I am bankrupt but spiritually I am the wealthiest man that I know. It seems to me that the adversary is continually running interference in every way possible and making sure that I am not advancing ahead financially too fast because he is trying to delay the publishing of this manuscript. But in this case again, all he is doing is allowing God's work to be accomplished as planned. And the longer and harder he works at his interference of God's plan for this book, the harder he will fall for all my testimonies will become as lethal weapons against him.

As I continue my journey, many find it hard to believe that I can be like I am. This helps me truly understand how much our world has been conditioned by the adversary. As natural as it is for me to do and respond in a godly way to just about everything, many find it very hard to grasp and truly understand why and how I am able to behave in such ways. Let the truth be known that it is all because of Jesus Christ who died for me. Had it not been for his death on the cross to redeem me from all my past sins, my present and all my future sins, all hope would be null and void and life would be meaningless. Jesus is and always will be the answer to everything and as I live and breath, I shall never forget his sacrifice for me, the sinner.

Almost on a daily basis now, the adversary has made his attacks on me more detailed, specific, and extremely targeted at me to the last minute on how, in my new strengthened faith in this journey, my God provides for me and takes care of me. In the past, the devil had a firm hand in directing me through life successfully in his worldly ways and would find hardly any resistance on my part. But now it is a three hundred and sixty degree difference in my ways because I have made God the center of my life daily. As much as he is tempting and trying to plant doubts in my mind as I continue to trust and believe that my God will always take care of me; I stand firm in my belief and I will continue always to make the ethical codes of God the center of everything that I do until the day I leave this earth.

My passion and understanding of God's love and ways are the most amazing thing that I have ever experienced and by far the absolute best ever. Some days are harder than others but my mind will stay always clear and my focus always on my God.

What would seem to others as pain and suffering, trials and tribulation, oppression, discomforts and torture, I see as being molded into perfection.

I recently got arrested and I was taken to jail by the Denver police department. They held me temporarily at a police substation for a couple hours. Then two officers came into my cell and asked me to stand up for a search of my body before they transported me to where I was to spend time locked up before I get to see the judge and be charged officially. These two officers treated me as inhumane as I have ever been treated in my life. I was placed in the back of a transport van-like vehicle made out of metal welded and bolted together with holes on the inner panel part of the box. As they drove me to my destination, they were telling jokes amongst themselves, dirty jokes — and laughing as if I, Eddy Colin, did not exist; as if they were transporting an animal and not a human being. They drove carelessly and never once looked back at me through their window in order to check on me as if they even cared. They drove so badly, I was being bounced around in that cage from side to side. When they would come to a traffic light or a stop sign, they would almost lock the breaks, and when taking off from those stops, they would just floor the gas. Through all this, I got bounced around pretty badly as those two officers laughed and used vulgar language.

Once settled in my cell I decided to abstain from food and fast for three days for this is the final chapter of this book. And my God will prevail for the truth is on my side. I am being accused of something that never happened, something that I did not do. And without getting into all the details, when they brought me in front the judge I pleaded not guilty. With the truth that I now live by, with God on my side, and having the Holy Spirit as my counselor, I set a jury trial of six and I am representing myself without any fear whatsoever, for God and the truth is with me. The trial date is May the twenty first, two thousand eight, and this will be my opening statement to the court and the jury:

Jury trial preparation for may 21ˢᵗ, 2008 @ 8:am

Ladies and gentlemen of the jury, I am just a simple God fearing man who is trying my best to abide by God's code of ethics as I try to help and assist those in need. What I am armed with today is the truth, my God's given code of ethics, my morals and the best justice system in the world. Our system may not be perfect, but it is still the best in the world bar none! You will have the opportunity to be part of something bigger then you have ever been before, for you are contributing in writing the conclusion of my book (My struggles, my bondage, and my freedom and deliverance). What you are contributing to is the conclusion of my journey and final chapter of my book. The truth must and will prevail. May the Holy Spirit guide you and give you insights and help you prove my innocence by finding me not guilty, for God himself is on trial. My book is about my deliverance from the bondage from the adversary on drugs and alcohol, and high blood pressure since 1994.

A few months before I got saved, I took in a single mom and her family as she had been without at job for several months. I let her live with me rent free right now because she has not had steady employment for awhile and has stayed without a job for as long as six months so far. I pay her rent, her phone bill, etc., to help out but she drinks all the time now. I still feel that there is hope on helping her beat this thing, but her mood changes all the time. The longer she stays without a drink, the worst it gets. Eventually, she breaks down and gets drunk and I never know which way she will come at me. Once she is drunk, she does not know when to stop drinking, and she will want to fight for she is out of control and can't think rationally. Per her counselor, she should not even have one drink because she does not know when to stop. Also per her counselor, she is bipolar and must go through a drug and alcohol program and take medications in order to get well. She must submit herself for breath and urine tests. How long can I endure this? I am not sure. But I want to be there for her and her kids because I want to help them have a life that they will not have without someone like me being there for

*them. I now live as a prisoner in my own
house, and I am afraid of what the next
made up story may be, and where I might
end up unjustly. Please help me fix this
grave injustice. I must and I will stay strong,
I will continue to pray to my God for
guidance and I believe with all my being
that the will of God as always will continue
to be done in my life as this final chapter
unveils the might of my creator, the God
above all gods. In the end, once this
injustice has been repaired and this case is
closed, we will all have learned that God
always has a plan and is ultimately in
charge of all aspects and details of our lives.
I am so honored that as bad as it seems for
me right now, that God chose me to
accomplish his work and it is truly a
privilege to have been chosen.*

My deepest level of understanding of my
Creator has allowed me to know and always
believe that I must make Him always the
center of my life and, even with the adversary
circling about and searching for weaknesses
to penetrate my armor or at least try to, I
remain steadfast in my belief and have stayed
anchored in my God for there is no other

way for me. I never once lost my courage nor did I lose my faith in the fact that my counselor, the Holy Spirit, has always been with me and would guide me through this jury trial all the way till the end. He has led me and guided me through my whole preparation for this trial, gave me all the right words to say when needed, and insured my readiness. I felt at peace all the way through the process and never once did I fear any defeat for I had the best counselor-at-law that money could buy and all it cost me was my faith and belief in Jesus Christ. My firm belief is that the absolute best place to be is under the wings of God for it is the safest place and the purest form of freedom.

The day before the jury trial was to start, the devil threw one more dart at me and things almost got out of hand with the single mom over almost nothing at all. Had the devil been successful, I in all probability would have missed my court date, would have been found in contempt of court, and would have been convicted; but I was immediately guided out of the situation by the Holy Spirit, who led me to safety. That night, the twentieth of May two thousand eight, I slept in my vehicle all night until 5 a.m. When I woke up, I was still mentally and physically ready and prepared to go to trial.

Upon arriving at the courthouse, I met with the district attorney, shared all that I had prepared for: files, subpoena of witnesses, 911 tapes, records etc... etc..., and three hours or so later, when my case was called, the district attorney for the city of Denver in charge of prosecuting me decided that they were not prepared to proceed with the trial, and based on all the new information that I had brought to light, they did not feel that they could win this case, and he (the district attorney) respectfully requested that the judge dismiss my case.

I believe that the presence of the Holy Spirit was in that courtroom that morning because with no objection from the judge, my case was dismissed once and for all. Praise be to my God for He is still as alive as ever and still on His throne today. The power of my God prevailed. When sometimes you see yourself in defeat, stay in your prayers continuously for God has already seen you on the other side of victory.

I know that God the Holy Spirit is within and my perfect reaction or response must also be harmonious with my Creator. One must be at peace first with oneself and know no boundary as you live a pure and graceful life with all of God's ethical codes and without any compromise. This way of life is the ultimate and purest for it will teach you to walk in perfect harmony with God the Holy Spirit. The Holy Spirit cannot and will never conform to our standards but we must conform ourselves to his standards if we are to ever attain perfection according to God's perfect will and standards.

The world as we know it, most will disagree that such relationship is possible and that is only because the adversary has a strong hold on this world and he knows that the time is drawing very near, and he is dreading his final days. Without a doubt, if God can use me in the manner in which He has been using me, after a twenty six year struggle and bondage from which He freed and delivered me, thus allowing the book of enlightenment to emerge in its proper time for the enlightenment and the deliverance of all who are now ready to be freed and delivered from the adversary the devil, imagine what my God can do through you.

My dear friends, I beg of you to not waste this life without understanding these words which I have been commissioned to pass on to you that you may know the gift that your God has for you. You must pray always, all the time, every time that you think of it, say a little prayer. No matter how insignificant it may seem to you, do not hesitate to just do it, for it matters. The devil will try to convince you that it seems crazy, that normal people don't act like that — and he will be right about that because "we are not like the others, we are God's people". Besides the life that my mother gave me, this fountain of knowledge that I have been given by my Creator is the absolute best thing that has ever happened to me, thus makes me the wealthiest man that I know personally.

But you must know that none of these words would signify anything if God had not given His only begotten son Jesus Christ as the ultimate sacrifice, with His death and shed blood on that rugged Roman cross for our past, present, and future sins; where once again He defeated the adversary, for our savior Jesus Christ rose again and conquered death. At that point our debt to the adversary was paid in full. The devil has no hold on us anymore.

My friends it is 8:24 a.m., Wednesday November twelve 2008. Immediately after my statement of how Jesus defeated the devil through His death on the cross and our debt to the adversary was paid in full, and that the devil had no hold on us anymore, I felt an evil presence in the room all around me. Goose bumps. My hair felt as if tingling. Surely the presence is here and very upset and once again trying to stop this book from emerging. I immediately went into my prayers and asked for the divine light of God to surround me, shield me and protect me from harm, and so it was done. The presence re-entered the room once again, stronger, and I felt that it was very angry and agitated. I repeated my prayer and this time I asked that the spirit be bonded down in the holy name of Jesus Christ and immediately the room was cleansed and purged of all that was unclean.

The power of prayer is totally amazing and real but you must have complete one hundred percent faith and believe in the empowerment, for once the devil was conquered through the death and resurrection of Jesus Christ, we became privileged children once again. But first we must truly embrace all that is good and follow the footsteps of Jesus Christ who is the way and the truth.

The question that hundreds of millions of people here on earth are asking every second that goes by: *Why am I here and what is my purpose?* There always seems to be a missing peace of the puzzle, an emptiness from deep within, a void that can't seem to be filled by anything — not the fame, not the women or the men that we chase after; not the drugs or the intoxicant we choose to put in our bodies, not all the pleasures of this world will satisfy this void and make you happy, for it only feeds it and magnifies it more and more. So what is the answer? Jesus says that first, you must deny yourself. He also says to pick up your cross and follow him for He is the way and the truth and that no one will enter the kingdom unless they go through Him.

I have often heard people say, "Well, it is not a perfect world!" I say to you that your own world guided by the Holy Spirit is in deed a perfect world, for the gray areas of the world today does not exist there. There will always be many situations where doubts will enter your mind, but you must always allow yourself to stay in the light and must be harmoniously in synchronization with your guide (the Holy Spirit), or you will create gray areas which will compromise everything that our God stands for, thus disrupting the union between you and the Holy Spirit. My friends, this perfect world of which I am speaking of is very real and the power is within all of us to live in it perfectly.

A year ago I said that I felt being the beginning of a new creation, a new evolution in the works, I now understand better and I have a clear picture of it for my guide, my counselor, the Holy Spirit, is one with me and I vow for as long as I am on this earth to abide by all that is good in the eyes of God my father, and there will and could never be another way for me to live on this earth because too much is at stake. Being in the automotive industry, recently (yes, I am working again) I was asked by a superior to perform an act that would have violated my godly code of ethics and, even though I knew that doing the right thing would cost me at least seven hundred dollars out of my pocket, I instinctively did the right thing and my action allowed the Holy Spirit to guide me in another direction, thus saving the car deal without any compromise where a gray area would have easily been created.

I must continue to allow the Holy Spirit to guide me for our God knows best what is and what is not good for us. I will never waiver from my faith and my belief in God.

In all of the United States of America we have used and abused our God given privileges so much. Compared to the rest of the world, obviously God has blessed us tremendously as a country, but we have so violated the rules and much of the ethical codes given to us by our Creator that we have come to the crossroads where we must either come clean with our God, correct all that has been violated in His eyes, and make atonements, or continue to live in the gray areas which will take us out of favor with our Creator.

For a fact, after having been in the car industry for twenty one years, and as I now live by different codes as a new creation of God, I find it very hard to continue to work in this industry for ninety nine percent of the time it's all gray areas. Most of the wealth accumulated by these giants has been accumulated through deceptions and tricks of the trade. Money has become their gods and no amount seems to be enough. The automotive industry is suffering the way it is and will continue to suffer until God separates those who will follow the true roads and those who will continue to follow the way of the adversary, the devil.

My good friends, I know one hundred percent that there is a big storm coming and you best get yourselves right with your Creator, for the time is closer then you think. In God's own perfect time will everything come to be or to past for He is the creator of all. There are those who may never make it on this side and experience the awesome presence of the Holy Spirit in their lives, and it saddens me so much to know of the sensational feelings and divine love in its purest form that they may never get to know. For those people, I will continually pray for their salvation before the window of opportunity for grace is permanently shut.

My unknown friends, I urge you, I beg of you, to please slow yourselves down and take your time to become imbued with these words of truth that I have been commissioned to pass on to you from the Divine, for your eternal lives depend on what you do with these words once they have been put upon your hearts.

At this time, I pray to our Creator to touch you in a very special way, that the Holy Spirit would descend upon you, open your hearts and minds, and help you to understand fully why it is not by coincidence that you have this book in your hands. May God grace you with a clear mind to comprehend the importance of these words now in your hands. Deep within my being, I know and I can feel something of great importance, something that will impact our civilization to its core, is about to take place and only those who are prepared and are sheltered under the wings of the Almighty God will emerge victorious out of it. Your days here on this earth are shorter then you think, and you need to pay attention to this call that God has just made to you; listen, listen closely and you will hear your Shepherd's voice. We must embrace all people as if they were our own, we must never allow our fear of the unknown to enslave us. Your minds must be open to limitless possibilities. Only then can we experience knowledge that is available and attainable by all of us. We are children of light, created by God, and we must return to the light — only then can we accomplish what the ancients have accomplished already.

Brothers and sisters, please allow the Holy Spirit to enter and become as one with you so you can experience pure love, happiness, humility and compassion as you have never ever experienced before. Only then can you have the peace and tranquility as you should.

I am here to tell you that God loves you more then you have ever imagined and there are many gifts that await you, but Jesus Christ is the answer and the way. Hypocrisy and deception seems to be as if normal these days. But I say to you, it will consume you in the end as a beast consumes its kill and satisfies its hunger. Do not allow yourself to be compromised for you already know that it only brings you temporary gains. Do not sell yourself so short for you already know that it is the wrong path and it only leads to self destruction. You cannot call yourself Godly and yet live in the gray areas of this world, for that will make you a hypocrite in the eyes of God. You must not surrender to Christ partially but completely, only then can you call yourself a true follower of Jesus Christ.

If you allow the Holy Spirit to truly guide you, everything will become easier and easier everyday and your guided journey will become as easy as the involuntary action of breathing. I know the God that I serve would never allow anyone to be lost for any length of time whatsoever. That is exactly why Jesus sent us the Holy Spirit to be our counselor and our guide, to walk with us as one so we can never go astray for too long and open the possibilities of us becoming hardened thus giving the adversary open season to hunt us down and destroy us. First you must believe without the shadow of a doubt that God is as real as you are here reading this book. Second you must understand and also believe that after the fall of man in the garden of Eden, we fell short of being worthy of the glory of God and we became enslaved to the adversary the devil. Third God loves us so much that He allowed His one and only son Jesus Christ to not just die for our sins, but went through atrocious pains and agonies, mocked, ridiculed and killed in the most horrific way, and became sin himself, just for us, in order so our debts to the adversary the devil was paid, and He cleared us of our debts forever.

My friends, that is pure unselfish love and compassion. This innocent man unselfishly and out of his own free will gave his own life for you and me so we could be free and clear of all our debts once and for all. If we could love one another half as much as Jesus loves us this world would be well on its way. We should rejoice and celebrate everyday while remembering the ultimate sacrifice ever made since the creation of the world and understand that the little things that we go through every day that seem so important are really not so important at all. We must try our hardest to stay focus on the true meaning of life itself and what we are going to do with our lives in order to secure eternal life to its fullest with our creator where there will be no pains, no suffering, no sorrow, no problems what so ever, a place to enjoy your love ones and everything that is good in the eyes of God our creator.

My friends, this God of ours is so awesome, he is and should always be the center of everything that we do all the time and there should never be any excuses or reasons why we as His own creation cannot have an intimate relationship and converse with Him at any time we desire to. We have so much resources in our God available to us all and yet we are not capitalizing on them. And I am not speaking of the materialistic things for the self. Once you are under the wings of God securely, you will understand more how it really works for you will have truly become a new creation guided by the Holy Spirit. The Holy Spirit was sent to us as our companion, as our guide and as our counselor to be within us always, He was promised and sent to us by our savior and redeemer Jesus Christ to keep us in the right path, the path that will lead us directly into his kingdom in heaven. But we must shed that old skin by washing ourselves in the blood of Christ and rid of our selfish nature and accept the whole world as our brothers and sisters, as our mothers and fathers. Only then can we have the peace, love, tranquility and true guidance that the Holy Spirit will give us.

If you knew that tonight would be your last night alive if you were to allow yourself to fall asleep and that your life depended on your keeping your eyes open until daylight, would you do everything you possibly could do to not allow yourself to fall asleep? Would you dedicate everything in your life to stay awake? Would you then pray with the utmost passion to God your creator to help you stay awake? To watch over you so you don't fall asleep for the last time and never to wake up again? My friends, life is a gift, a fragile gift that we must learn to cherish and protect everyday while here on earth for this is the learning center where we condition and prepare ourselves so we may be able to spend eternity with our father God forever and ever. Life here on earth is just a flash in comparison to what awaits us in heaven.

If you have this book in your hands right now and reading it, God the Holy Spirit is trying to press upon you the urgency of living a clean, pure and guided life by the Holy Spirit. To truly understand the transformation that has taken place in my own life, and to believe how the Holy Spirit works in us, it is imperative if you have not done so already that you read about my struggles, my bondage and my freedom and deliverance by God at the beginning of this book before you continue reading further. Once you have read about my freedom and deliverance, there will be no doubts in your minds about the power of our Creator and how much we mean to Him as His own creation, and His wish for us not to perish but be saved.

Earlier in this book, I mentioned that there was a storm coming and that no one would be safe unless they sought shelter under the wings of God himself. These days now, as I watch all the world events — the cyclone that has claimed hundreds of thousands of lives, the devastating earthquake that has claimed so many thousands of lives, how hard the United States has been getting hit with this frightening economy, and, for the first time ever, I believe we are seeing a presidential election in the great United States taking a turn like it has never taken before, lately I have been feeling very unrested and I truly feel that this great storm of which I mentioned may be much closer than I think. Brothers and sisters, <u>I beg of you!</u> Pay close attention to these words that I am revealing to you and get yourselves under His wings right now, for your eternal lives are all at stake.

If you look at how things have been in the world, or I should say how things are in the world today, a person without the divine guidance of the Holy Spirit and knowledge of the truth may easily conclude that the devil was not defeated at all, specially as they observe the world around them and see people who are known to be ungodly, selfish, the kind of people who are known to be ill-mannered and arrogant, who on a daily basis are taking advantage of any and all opportunities and hurting others without thinking twice of how bad their behaviors are leaving marks that are effecting so many lives negatively and permanently. Under no circumstance that you are to allow the devil to trick you into such way of thinking for he is the master of trickery.

I have stretched my mind to attempt for a moment to figure out how any one person could even for a brief moment say that: if the devil had really been defeated, then why is it that things are as bad as they are? And why is it that all around us we are seeing evidence that the devil is in charge? Well, I say to you as God is my witness! I shall be living proof for all who are ready and are willing to listen to their hearts that the same God who created the universe also created us in His own image, that's how much He loves us. He also lost us for a while to the adversary the devil when Adam and Eve gave up their rights in the garden of Eden; but being God, he had also set a plan in motion to redeem us before we were even created.

My good friends, every day should be a celebration for life is most precious. Our redemption started with one life and through the birth of that child, God won our freedom back from the devil once and for all. The next time you celebrate Christmas, give it all you got and take the time to seriously know that you are celebrating the birth of the Christ, the one who gave up his own life so you and I may be here today. I personally make everyday my Christmas because I love him more than anything in this world, I shall continue to love him until the day I leave this earth.

Knowing what is right is one thing, knowing what is right and abiding by it in doing all that is right takes a perfect union with the Holy Spirit your counselor and we can never do it alone. There are two statements that remain with me and are always in my thoughts: (1) *I will never leave you nor forsake you!* (2) *fear not for I am with you always!* One can continue to question with doubts or one can simply allow the guidance of the Holy Spirit to just flow without resistance and just believe that God our father always wants the best for us, and someday it will all be understood clearly.

I say that something is very wrong with our world when an elderly person prefers to struggle to walk on an icy sidewalk in negative degree temperatures instead of accepting a ride from me to get her home safely. I dream of a world where all thoughts and acts are purely unselfish and are out of genuine love, where the God kind of love dominates all, where none of us ever have to wonder about right or wrong because wrong no longer exist.

My quest for the rest of my days here on earth is to continually seek and gain greater knowledge from the wisest of all, the one who lives within me; the one who counsels me every second of my new created life for which I am so thankful. To truly understand as a new created being, it takes the total care of the Holy Spirit within and understanding that is the beginning of my wisdom. I passionately love all that is of God my father but all else effect and hurt me deeply in the manner that one feels pains when the physical body is bruised; it also pains my heart and soul to see most of the world today as it is.

My friends, we have so much work to do before we can even come close the level of understanding of which I am speaking of! Many will be left behind unless they take the first step into their life of freedom and every second wasted is precious.

Again I say to you my dearest brothers and sisters, do not throw away your eternity for the temporary things that the devil our adversary has been glamorously advertizing to you all. Take charge of your own life by asking Jesus Christ to come into your life and save you by accepting you as you are right now, and surrender your life so you also may become a new creation in the family of God as I have. We are so much more then the devil has been tricking us into believing for all this time, but now our eyes have been opened to limitless divine possibilities for we are all children of light.

The fact is that none of us will ever know for sure the time when our number will come up once called. We best be ready to answer about our lives here on earth for which we are accountable. There will be no shortcuts, no gray areas. It should be something to look forward to and not have any doubts what so ever about. Being in accordance with the Holy Spirit every time/all the time is an extremely fragile balance and I cannot even imagine a life without my counselor from within to guide me in the right direction every step I take.

As a true student of wisdom, "divine wisdom" as I look into the ungodly eyes of this world in which we live, I pray to my God for a divine revival and intervention as I thank Him that the doors of grace are still open for if they were to close right now, most of the world would perish, and my observation is based on divine enlightenment. Everything about this world in which we live is totally superficial and most of it, including those who are abusing and enjoying such things, are but temporary things; meanwhile the adversary the devil is in the background celebrating the downfall of all those involved.

I am on the final stretch to finishing this book of enlightenment and my God has prepared me extremely well to start witnessing for him so many may have a chance to know that it is not too late for them to be saved, for Jesus has already paid the price on the cross for all of us and our debt to the adversary is paid in full.

I had a vision of a place, like an old beautiful ancient country, mountainous and very plush, I know and feel deep within my being that this place exists and has always been. Very grand with two massive pillars, overwhelmingly large, stony adjoining walls on either side of the pillars but no security gate to prevent unauthorized entry, for one can only enter if you are pure. At the bottom of the steps is the Master, Shepherd of all shepherds, the Grand Master of all. His body glows in an inviting and peaceful manner as He weeps for His lost children knowing that it is time.

My friends, God is calling you with one final invitation to come home to Him, and He weeps for your return. Please, I beg of you, if you can find your way anywhere close to home, you will see Him at the bottom of the steps near the gate. He is still full of grace as ever. He loves you unconditionally, regardless of how dirty you may feel that you are right now, no matter how great you may feel that your sins may be, the blood of His son Jesus Christ is strong enough to cleanse you once and for all. He is calling you today to come home. All you have to do is accept His son Jesus Christ as your personal savior and lord and immediately your eyes will be opened to the final road that will surely lead you to the bottom of those steps, and you shall see Him, for His body glows in a peaceful and inviting manner, and you shall surely feel and know that you are home.

My dear brothers and sisters, as I live and breathe this day, I in truth say to you that the journey starts at the foot of the cross. All the load that presses heavily on your shoulders right now can be brought and left right here at the foot of the very cross where Jesus died for you and I and paid for all our past, present, and future sins once and for all. He is calling you to come to the foot of the cross with all your heavy loads that you are no longer able to carry, just lean over and drop them off right here and right now.

On your knees, ask Jesus to take it all for you — tell Him that you are surrendering all to Him right now and to wash you of all your sins — and I assure you that it shall be done instantly. As God is my witness, I promise you that it is that simple, because I have been there at the foot of that same cross and have left twenty six years of very heavily soiled and displeasing loads at that very same place. I say to you today and now that there is no one too young and no one too old, or beyond the reach of my God.

My redemption would not even be possible had it not been for the death of my lord and savior Jesus Christ on that rugged Roman cross over two thousand years ago, when all my sins were paid for in full as He conquered death through His resurrection three days later. I have found true happiness at the age of forty-eight, and God is the reason for my happiness. The peace and happiness from within me is nothing like I have ever experienced since my life here on this earth has began and I realized that the only way for one to ever experience such peacefulness, such happiness and tranquility, is to allow the Holy Spirit to guide you in not almost everything that you do but everything that you do always/ all the time. The union will become so distinguishable that others will want to know more about what has happened to you, which will open the door for your testimony on God's behalf and since it will all be the truth, and since you are guided by the Holy Spirit, it should be extremely comfortable for you telling those who want to know.

Everyday that I live and breathe on this earth, I shall always remember of my freedom and deliverance from my struggles and my bondage with drugs and alcohol where the adversary had me bonded down for twenty-six years. I have and will continue to dedicate my life here to the service of my one and only God, my creator, my everything; and my goal is to do everything I possibly can do to reach as many as I can and tell them of this infinite supreme treasure that I have acquired, and how anxious I am to share it with all who are willing to accept it for free — which means they don't ever have to repay back anything, for everything has already been taken care of by the one whose name is Jesus Christ.

My biggest hope is, and I pray to God, that you can all be given spiritual insight to everything that I have put down for you to read and truly understand it all. This is the kind of journey that every man should anticipate and have dreams of being on everyday of his or her life until that day comes when he or she is actually at a point to be able to enjoy having the presence of God in their lives everyday and enjoy it all the time.

I look forward to the twists and turns everyday now, For I know and feel more secured about my future. It feels so good and I am so privileged that God is using me and allowing me to feel, to see and experience his true ways at work through me, and being used as a tool to get these words to all who are ready to be enlightened.

Today, in my vision, I saw myself laying in an old coffin made out of tree trunk tied together with straw rope, and I saw myself emerging as a new creation clothed in a white robe carrying a long staff as if I am starting on a new journey. I know without a doubt that the Holy Spirit is within to guide me on this unknown journey. I exhort to you to join me on this new journey — a journey I am taking, still drug and alcohol free.